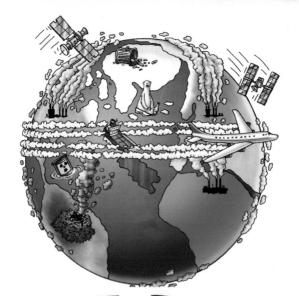

PLANET
IN
PERIL!

ANITA GANERI
ILLUSTRATED BY MIKE PHILLIPS

Consultant: Peter Littlewood,
Director of the Young People's Trust for the Environment

This book is made from 115 gsm uncoated, FSC-compliant paper.
The cover is made from 250 gsm recycled board. The inks are vegetable
based; not made from petroleum products. It has been printed in the EU
to reduce its impact on the environment.

Scholastic Children's Books,
Euston House, 24 Eversholt Street,
London, NW1 1DB, UK

A division of Scholastic Ltd
London ~ New York ~ Toronto ~ Sydney ~ Auckland
Mexico City ~ New Delhi ~ Hong Kong

Editorial Director: Lisa Edwards
Senior Editor: Jill Sawyer

First published in the UK by Scholastic Ltd, 2008

Text copyright © Anita Ganeri, 2008
Illustrations copyright © Mike Phillips, 2008
Colour by Tom Connell
All rights reserved

ISBN 978 1407105 77 2

Printed and bound in Germany by GGP Media GmbH, Poessneck

2 4 6 8 10 9 7 5 3 1

CONTENTS

INTRODUCTION

To you, Planet Earth is home, sweet home. The centre of your universe. There's nowhere else quite like it, you'd reckon. And you'd be right. Dead right. Forget boring old Mercury or Jupiter. Never mind dull-as-ditchwater Venus or Mars. It's official! Our very own Earth's the only place we know of where it's possible for horrible humans to live. There's just one teeny problem. Horrible humans have been living on the Earth for centuries and the exhausted Earth's starting to feel the strain. Yep, horrible humans are making the Earth seriously sick. Cars and factories are belching ghastly gases into the atmosphere, making the Earth worryingly warm. And that's not all. We're also wasting vital resources like fuel and water, chopping down forest-loads of trees, and generally making a mind-boggling mess of things. And with more people being born every minute, the planet is under pressure like never before. But before you think, 'Hm, perhaps Mercury doesn't sound so bad after all', and hop on the first spaceship outta here, DON'T PANIC! This horribly useful handbook contains everything you'll need to save the planet ... before it's too late.

So, read on to find out…
- the size of your carbon footprint
- how to run your car on chocolate
- how to turn elephant poo into paper
- why giving up baths is good news for the planet
- why eating crisps is bad news for orang-utans

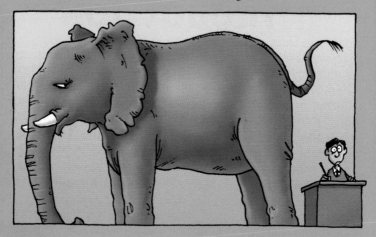

Yep, this handy book is packed with hundreds of earth-shattering hints and tips for going green. But we're not talking green with envy when you see your friend's new trainers. Or green around the chops after scoffing down too much of your granny's double chocolate-chip trifle with cream. Going green means living in a way that doesn't do the planet so much harm. Don't worry. You don't suddenly have to start munching on lentils (or even give up crisps completely). Though you might need to get used to turning the tap off when you're cleaning your teeth. Still keen to give green living a go? Well, you'd better get your skates on. Things are warming up … fast.

TOO HOT TO HANDLE?

Reckon you know what's the biggest threat facing the planet? Go on, have a guess. No, it isn't your little sister, even when she's pinching your stuff. Getting any warmer? Well, you soon might be. The answer's called global warming and you could soon be feeling the heat. OK, so this might not seem likely if you're reading this on a freezing cold day. But horribly clued-up scientists say the evidence is everywhere. Across the globe, glaciers are melting, and the ice at the North Pole is shrinking fast. And that's just for starters. (You can read about other sweltering side effects of global warming later on in this chapter.) Most of these brainy boffins agree that global warming's here to stay. What's more, it's horrible humans who are largely to blame. They just don't know how quickly it'll happen or how much warmer the Earth will get. So will the Earth eventually get too hot to handle? Or is there anything you can do before it's too late? You'd better keep reading. This chapter's packed with horribly green and helpful tips on how to cool things down a bit.

EARTH ALERT FILE

Name: GLOBAL WARMING
What it is: THE WAY THE EARTH'S TEMPERATURE IS WARMING UP

HOW IT HAPPENS:

1 Greenhouse gases in the atmosphere trap heat coming from the Sun. They work a bit like the glass in a greenhouse, that's how they got their name.

2 Humans are pumping tonnes more of these ghastly gases into the atmosphere. They mostly come from factories, cars, planes and lorries, and burning down rainforests.

3 Problem is, the amount of gases is growing too fast because of horrible human activities. And too much heat is being trapped, putting the planet at risk of roasting.

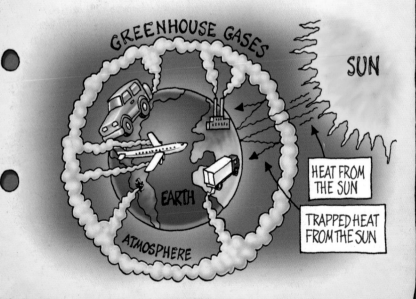

GREENHOUSE GASES

SUN

EARTH

ATMOSPHERE

HEAT FROM THE SUN

TRAPPED HEAT FROM THE SUN

Global warming facts:

- Some global warming's good for you. If there weren't any greenhouse gases, the Earth would be far too f–f–f–freezing cold for anything to live on.
- Fossil fuels* – coal, oil and gas – are mainly to blame for greenhouse gases. They're burned in power stations and factories, and in our cars and planes.
- By the year 2050, scientists reckon, there'll be twice as much of the ghastly greenhouse gas carbon dioxide in the atmosphere as now.
- All these gases might warm up the Earth by about 5°C in the next 100 years. Which might not sound much to you but it could be curtains for the planet.

*They're called 'fossil' fuels because they're mainly made from plants that bloomed around the time of the dinosaurs, millions of years ago.

Greenhouse gas rogues' gallery

Name: Carbon dioxide
Distinguishing features: Invisible; odourless
Sources:
- Burning fossil fuels
- Burning rainforests
- Cement making
- Draining and burning peatlands

It's a gas:
- Humans pump a gigantic 26 gigatonnes (26 billion tonnes) of carbon dioxide into the atmosphere each year.
- Burning one paltry litre of petrol adds over 2 kg of carbon dioxide to the air.
- Carbon dioxide's the gas that humans and animals breathe out.

Name: Methane
Distinguishing features: Invisible; odourless
Sources:

- Coal mining/drilling for oil and gas
- Rice paddy fields
- Rubbish dumps and landfill sites
- Melting permafrost
- Cows' burps and farts (also sheep, goats, camels and buffalo)

It's a gas:

- It's also called swamp gas because it's formed when bacteria break down the dead swamp plants and animals.
- Humans pump about 500 million tonnes of methane into the air each year.
- Cows burp out more than 200,000 tonnes of methane a day. It's made when bacteria break down the cows' chewed-up food.

BURP!

Name: Nitrous oxide
Distinguishing features: Invisible; slightly sweet smell
Sources:

- Fertilizers used on farmland
- Human and animal sewage
- Burning fossil fuels

It's a gas:
- Humans are pumping a massive 7–13 million tonnes of nitrous oxide into the air each year.
- Nitrous oxide's also found naturally in the oceans and soil where bacteria break down the gas nitrogen.
- It's the third largest greenhouse gas after carbon dioxide and methane.

Name: Fluorocarbons
Sources:

- Fridges and air conditioning
- Aerosol spray cans
- Aluminium making

It's a gas:
- The three worst kinds are CFCs (chlorofluorocarbons), HCFCs (hydrochlorofluorocarbons) and HFCs (hydrofluorocarbons).
- A molecule of CFC is 10,000 times better at trapping heat than a molecule of carbon dioxide.
- CFCs also destroy the ozone layer – a gassy blanket that protects the Earth from the Sun's harmful ultraviolet rays.

EARTH—SHATTERING FACT

Global warming could be a whole lot worse without carbon sinks. But they're not the sort of sinks you wash in. Remember those? These sinks are actually the oceans and rainforests. Together, they soak up about half of all the carbon dioxide that's pumped into the atmosphere. How? Well, titchy sea plants and towering rainforest trees use tonnes of carbon dioxide to grow. Trouble is, global warming's putting the sinks under serious strain. As the oceans warm up, sea plants can't soak up so much gas. And rainforest trees are being chopped down at an alarming rate. What's worse, when the trees are burned, they release millions more tonnes of carbon dioxide to add to the atmosphere's load.

Five burning questions about climate change

Q 1: Is climate change the same as global warming?

A: Not really. Global warming means the way the Earth's getting warmer because of things horrible humans are doing. Climate change is the way global warming seems to be changing weather patterns around world. Worried scientists reckon the climate is changing faster than at any time in the last 10,000 years. Some places are becoming wetter or drier. Or stormier. And that's not all... (Read on to find out about more alarming side effects.)

Q 3: How can scientists tell?

A: Curious scientists track down clues telling them what the climate was like in the past. Then they compare their findings to what they know about today's climate. These cunning climate clues include:

- Ice cores: Long sticks of ice, like giant ice lollies, drilled out of glaciers and ice sheets. By counting the layers of ice, scientists can tell how old the ice is. Air bubbles trapped in the ice contain traces of ancient greenhouse gases. An ice core they dug up in Antarctica showed there's now more carbon dioxide and methane in the atmosphere than at any time in the last 650,000 years. Core blimey.

- Tree rings: By counting the rings in a slice of tree trunk, scientists can tell how old the tree is. A tree grows a new ring every year and the weather affects how it grows. The different sizes and shapes of the rings tell scientists about changes in temperatures and precipitation (the posh name for rain and snow).

- Ocean sediment: Sediment's the muddy sludge covering the sea bed. It's chock-full of crushed-up seashells built by ancient sea creatures, as well as bits of soil and rock washed from the land. From the sediment, scientists can tell how salty the water was, what temperature it was, how much rain fell and even the direction and intensity of wind.

Q 4: Can the climate change naturally?

A: Sure thing. The climate's warmed up and cooled down many times in the Earth's history. And it's happened because of things like changes in the way the Earth spins round the Sun and violently erupting volcanoes. Take Tambora in Indonesia. When this violent volcano blew its top in 1815, it chucked so much gas, dust and ash into the air, it blocked the Sun and cooled the Earth by 1°C for over a year. In the USA, there was even snow in the middle of June. Each year, volcanoes blast millions of tonnes of carbon dioxide into the air – adding to global warming. But before you think horrible humans are off the hook, that's still only about a hundredth of what humans are releasing.

Q 5: So, what's the big deal, then?

A: You might think global warming sounds great. After all, scientists estimate the Earth will only get a few degrees warmer and who's moaning about that? It'd be like summer all year round. Bliss! But you'd be wrong. Forget lazing about on the beach, slapping on sun cream and slurping ice cream. Global warming is no summer holiday. Here are some of its more sinister side effects...

OOOPS!

Six sweltering side effects

Seas are getting warmer...

Bad news for many sea animals who can't adapt to the warmer water, but good news for jellyfish. They're blooming in the sizzling seas, forming swarms millions of jellyfish strong. Trouble is, the peckish jellyfish are also gobbling up precious fish stocks, so you could say global warming's starting to sting.

Sea levels are rising...

By the year 2100, the sea level might be over a metre higher than it is today. That's because global warming is melting the ice at the perishing poles. And when sea water warms up, it expands (gets bigger), sending sea level rising even more. Several islands in the Pacific Ocean have already vanished under the waves and many more may soon follow. Low-lying countries and places along the coast are also at risk of fatal flooding.

BEAR-LY A NIBBLE!

Glaciers and ice sheets are shrinking...

And it's already happening across the globe. Take the groovy glaciers on the Andes Mountains in South America. In the last ten years, the colossal Chacaltaya glacier in Bolivia has shrunk to half its size and could have melted completely by the year 2010. The gigantic sheet of ice capping Greenland is the size of France and Spain put together. Trouble is, it's starting to thin round the edges but worse might be to come. Scientists reckon that, if all of this ice melted, sea level would soar by a catastrophic 7 metres.

Polar bears are starving...

They're horribly cute and furry, and they look dead cool on Christmas cards. But polar bears are skating on seriously thin ice. In spring and summer, hungry bears hunt seals on the ice covering the Arctic Ocean. But the ice is melting earlier each year, making it harder for the bears to find food. Unless they can adapt to hunt on land, the bears' future looks seriously bleak. They're likely to be extinct in the wild by the year 2050.

The weather's getting wilder...

Freaky things are happening to the weather. And it's set to get worse. Some parts of the world are getting wetter, with heavier downpours of rain. Other places are getting drier, with more droughts drying up water supplies and causing crops to fail. Killer heatwaves are another hazard. In 2003, around 35,000 people died from heatstroke as temperatures soared across Europe. And that's not all. Hair-raising hurricanes are set to get stronger, last longer and hit places that haven't even heard of hurricanes before.

Deadly diseases are spreading...

Deadly diseases like malaria and yellow fever are spread by mosquitoes and kill millions of people each year. These murderous mossies love lurking in nice, warm places so global warming can't come too soon for them. Trouble is, as the world warms up, the mossies are starting to strike in places that were too cold for them to live in before...

Serious about saving the planet? The first thing horrible humans need to do is cut down the amount of greenhouse gases we're pumping into the overloaded atmosphere. You might not think you can do much, but every little helps. First you need to work out your 'carbon footprint' – that's how much carbon dioxide you're producing when you watch telly, cook your tea or fly off on holiday. Then you can set about changing your shoe size. Check out the websites at the back of this book to find out what to do.

EARTH–SHATTERING FACT

Thank your lucky stars you don't live on Shishmaref, a tiny island between Alaska and Siberia. Because of global warming, the islanders face a horribly rocky future. Each winter, the sea round the island freezes and the ice saves the island from storms. But the freeze is happening later and later, leaving the island to be lashed by winds and waves. Several of the islanders' houses have already been washed into the sea ... leaving them with no choice. They've voted to leave the island and move to a new village on the mainland.

GLOBAL WARMING SURVIVAL GUIDE

Grow your own fruit and veg

That way, you'll cut down on the number of kilometres your food has to travel from where it's grown to your plate. And that'll save tonnes of greenhouse-gas-guzzling fuel which is used to drive or fly the food around the world.

Plant a tree

As trees make food, their leaves soak up carbon dioxide from the air. And get this. In its lifetime, a single tree can soak up a whole tonne of the ghastly gas. So planting a tree's a horribly green thing to do.

ABOUT TIME!

Plant a roof

Top your roof with a layer of grass and pop in a few plants and shrubs. Don't forget to water your roof regularly. Your green roof won't only be pretty to look at. It'll also stop your house warming up or cooling down so quickly, so you won't need your heating or air-conditioning on as much. And this'll save precious energy (made from fossil fuels) and cut carbon dioxide.

Wear green

Next time you're shopping for new clothes, pick some that won't damage the planet. Cotton might be cool but it needs enormous amounts of energy, water and harmful chemicals to make it grow. Choose clothes made from something like hemp instead. Hemp is a plant that's easy to grow organically (that means without using chemicals).

Stop playing snooker

Many snooker cues are made from wood from rare rainforest trees. As you know, rainforests soak up loads of carbon dioxide but, sadly, they're being chopped down at an alarming rate. So, if you're shopping for snooker cues, look for wood that comes from sustainable forests. That means forests where chopped-down trees are replaced.

Adopt a glacier

Go up to a glacier and give it a hug. OK, so you'll have to use your imagination for this one. You can choose from glaciers at the parky Poles or slithering down freaky peaks around the globe. Monitor your frosty friend regularly to check for signs that it's shrinking. Don't worry, you won't be alone. Scientists are  using satellites to watch the world's glaciers. They hope that encouraging people to get to know glaciers better might persuade them to go green.

SURVIVAL TIP

Scientists have various crackpot schemes for getting rid of carbon dioxide. Like dumping tonnes of iron in the sea. They hope the iron will help tiny sea plants to bloom so they'll soak up thousands of tonnes of the gas. Will this potty plan actually work? Or will it do more harm than good? At the moment, no one really knows.

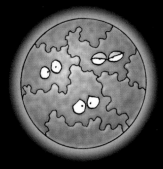

RUNNING OUT OF STEAM

Picture the scene. It's been a gruelling day at school and you've just got home. You're about to raid the fridge for a nourishing snack and settle down in front of the telly. So far, so good. Then suddenly you're transported back in time over 150 years and there isn't any telly or fridge. In fact, there's no electricity so you'll be doing your homework by candlelight. Don't bother trying to pop to the shops. You'll have to walk because there aren't any buses or cars. Sounds like a nightmare? Well, it could come true again. More than 1 million tonnes of fossil fuels are burned EVERY HOUR around the world in power stations (to generate electricity), factories and cars. Burning them belches out loads of greenhouse gases but that's not the only downside. Horrible humans are using fossil fuels so fast that they're running out. The race is on to find cleaner, longer-lasting sources of energy, not to mention ways of cutting down the enormous amount of energy we're using. Otherwise we might find ourselves well and truly in the dark.

EARTH ALERT FILE

Name: OIL AND GAS
What they are: KINDS OF FOSSIL FUELS

HOW THEY FORMED:

1 Millions and millions of years ago, the sea was full of tiny animals and plants.

2 When they died, they sank to the sea bed and were buried under layers of sand and mud.

3 The sand and mud turned into rock and squashed their rotting bodies into oil and gas.

Oil and gas facts:

● They're pumped out of the ground by an oil or gas rig, then piped to a refinery.

● Oil is made into petrol and diesel for cars and kerosene for plane engines, plastics, paints, medicines and fuel for power stations where electricity's made.

● Gas is used for cooking and heating our homes, and in power stations.

● There's only enough gas left to last another 60 years and enough oil for another 45.

EARTH ALERT FILE

Name: COAL
What it is: A KIND OF FOSSIL FUEL

HOW IT FORMED:

1 Millions and millions of years ago, the Earth was covered in swampy forests.
2 The forest trees died and, ever so slowly, rotted away...
3 ...leaving mainly the black carbon that makes coal behind.

Coal facts:
• It's dug out of rocks near the surface or deep underground in coal mines.
• It's one of the main fuels burned in power stations to make electricity.
• It's also been used as a fuel for cooking and heating for at least 10,000 years.
• There's enough coal left to last for about another 300 years. Possibly.

HORRIBLE HEALTH WARNING

Apart from ghastly greenhouse gases, there's another serious side effect of burning fossil fuels. They spew out clouds of foul fumes which poison the air you breathe. Some of these fumes mix with water droplets in the clouds and fall back to Earth as acid rain. OK, acid rain's only as acidic as vinegar so it's not likely to harm you. But it's fatal for fish and trees. In Europe, whole forests are being killed off and thousands of lakes have already lost all of their fish.

THIS IS VERY FISHY!

Six kinds of renewable* energy you might want to try at home

1 Solar energy

What it is: Energy that comes from the Sun as heat and light

How it works: Stick some solar panels on your roof to catch the Sun's heat for heating water. Or build a solar power station, where you can turn sunlight into electricity. The biggest solar power station's in the Mojave Desert, USA, where it's sunny all year round. There's even talk of building solar power stations in space.

---

* Renewable means a kind of energy you can make more and more of so it won't run out.

Pros:

• It's clean and there's plenty of it. The solar energy hitting the Earth is 10,000 times as much as we need.

• It's brilliant in far-flung places where it's difficult to get electricity.

Cons:

• Catching solar energy's horribly costly.

• It's brilliant in far-flung places … as long as they're SUNNY!

SURVIVAL TIP

Is it a sunny day where you live? Well, why not cook your tea outside? But forget boring old barbecues. Grab yourself a solar cooker and stick some grub inside. Then go off and do something else for a couple of hours and when you get back, tuck in. In hot countries like those in Asia or Africa, solar cooking could soon be all the rage. What's so brilliant about it? In these countries, millions of people rely on firewood for cooking their food. So solar cooking won't just stop people having to walk for miles. It'll help save forests as well. Burning wood also pumps out greenhouse gases but guess what? Yep, solar cooking's pollution free. What's more, the Sun* costs nothing so a solar cooker is horribly cheap to run. Boiled egg, anyone?

*Unfortunately, if it's cloudy, you're stuffed.

2 Geothermal energy

What it is: Energy from heat deep beneath the Earth

How it works: Masses of red—hot, molten (melted) rock lies underground. In some places, this superhot rock is very close to the surface. Why not tap into it for heating water for washing and turning into electricity? Hot stuff.

Pros:
• There's so much heat inside the Earth, it could last for millions of years.
• It's quite easy to harness by pumping cold water into the ground and waiting for it to warm up. Then you pump it back to the top.

Cons:
• It's fine in places like New Zealand, Japan and Iceland where you've got hot rocks right under your feet but not so convenient if you live somewhere that's stone cold.
• If pipes have to be drilled deep underground, it can cause pollution.

3 Wind energy

What it is: Power from the blowing wind

How it works: You'll need a wind turbine for this one. It's a tall pole with blades, a bit like a high-tech windmill. The wind sends the blades spinning round. As they spin, the blades operate a generator where the wind's energy is turned into electricity. It'll blow you away.

Pros:
• Wind's likely to be pretty widespread wherever you live.
• Experts reckon, by 2040, 12 per cent of the world's electricity could be down to a case of wind.

Cons:
• Some people think wind turbines are horribly ugly and spoil the view.
• A wind farm (that's a group of turbines) big enough to power a city might take up valuable (real) farmland space.

4 Hydroelectric power

What is it: Power from raging river water

How it works: You build a dam across a river to block its flow. Then let the water flow through the dam. It'll spin the blades of a turbine wheel and, in turn, work a generator to make electricity. You just go with the flow.

Pros:
- Once a dam is built, it's very cheap and clean to make.
- It's already responsible for up to a fifth of the world's electricity.

Cons:
- Homes and fields may have to be flooded when dams are built.
- The river's natural flow gets muddled, disturbing animals and plants.

33

5 Wave/tidal energy

What is it: Energy from the waves and tides

How it works:

a) Waves: You chuck a couple of ducks into the sea, then watch them bob up and down with the waves. This bobbing turns mini-turbines inside them and makes electricity. (Note: they're not real ducks. That would be cruel. They're special devices that look a bit like ducks.)

b) Tides: You build a massive barrier called a tidal barrage. It traps water at high tide. When the tide goes out, the water rushes out through turbines in the barrage. And they turn energy from the water into electricity.

Pros:

• Waves and tides hold huge amounts of energy and there's plenty of it to go round.
• You know when the tides are going to happen, day in, day out.

Cons:

•Tidal barrages are costly to build and can damage the landscape and local wildlife.
• Wave and tide power's all very handy, but only if you happen to live by the coast.

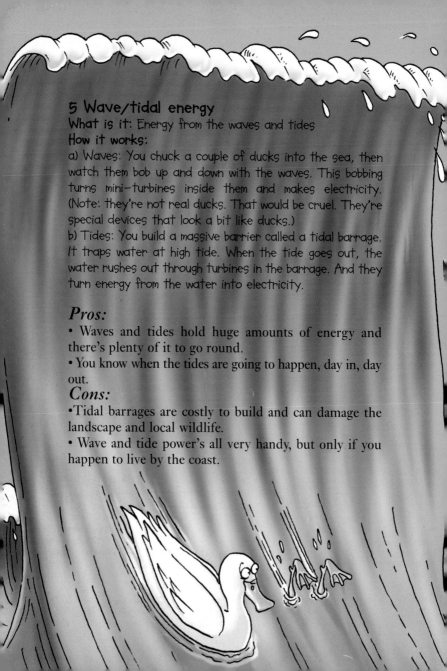

6 Nuclear energy

What is it: Energy made by splitting atoms* of uranium** apart
How it works: You build a nuclear power station for splitting the atoms. Use the huge amounts of heat this gives off to boil some water. Then use the steam from the water to drive giant turbines and generate electricity. Save some of your nuclear power for running your space probe or submarine.

Pros:
• It doesn't pump out greenhouse gases or cause acid rain.
• You can get 2 million times more energy from a lump of uranium than a lump of coal.

Cons:
• Power stations create radioactive waste that's deadly for tens of thousands of years.
• It's horribly costly to keep safe and very nasty accidents can happen.

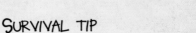

SURVIVAL TIP

If splitting atoms sounds far too tiring, and you don't live anywhere near the sea, why not try making fuels from plants and animals instead? They're called biofuels and some scientists think they're the best thing since sliced bread. What on Earth's got scientists so excited? Well, while burning biofuels gives out carbon dioxide, it's balanced out by the amount of gas soaked up by the plants when they grow. Would you be-leaf it?

*Atoms are mind-bogglingly minuscule particles that make up, well, everything.
** Uranium is a silvery-white metal that's mined from underground rocks.

Barmy biofuels quiz

Some seriously strange things have been turned into biofuels. But which of these freaky-sounding fuels do you think is too weird to work?

1 Sugar cane. Yes/No
2 Algae. Yes/No
3 Dead flies. Yes/No
4 Chocolate. Yes/No
5 Chopsticks. Yes/No
6 Chip fat. Yes/No

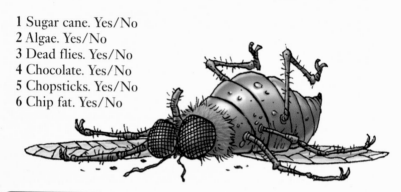

Answers:

Astonishingly, the answer to all of them is … YES!

1 The bits of sugar cane left over from making sugar are brewed up to make a biofuel called ethanol. In Brazil, about 4 million cars fill up with ethanol instead of petrol. Another million have a mixture of ethanol and petrol in their tanks.

2 Algae are tiny, fast-blooming plants that grow in seawater and ponds. Some green-fingered scientists are experimenting with sprouting algae in specially designed bags. The idea's to filter out the algae and burn them in an engine to make electricity.

3 Scientists have been busy building a robot that turns dead flies into electricity. And it got off to a flying start. Earlier, the same brainy boffins designed a robot that ran on slugs. But, guess what? Yep, it was too sluggish to get very far.

4 In 2007, a lorry from England tasted the sweet smell of success. It drove a staggering 8,500 kilometres to Timbuktu and back. The whole tasty trip was powered by 2,000 litres of biofuel, made from a mouth-watering 4,000 kg of choccie (think 80,000 yummy chocolate bars).

5 The Japanese chuck out millions of chopsticks each year, equal to a whopping 90,000 tonnes of wood. So green-thinking cities in Japan are setting up special chopstick bins where people can stick their, er, sticks. The plan's to collect the chopsticks up and change them into biofuel.

6 A company in England collects fat from local fish and chip shops and changes it into fuel for cars. This chip fat fuel works surprisingly well and, so far, the only problem has been a slight whiff of frying coming from the car's exhaust pipe.

HORRIBLE HEALTH WARNING

Some scientists say biofuels aren't as green as they're cracked up to be. For a start, the plants used to make them needs loads of space to grow. Huge patches of precious rainforests have already being razed to the ground to make way for massive sugar cane, palm oil and soya farms. And fields used for growing vital food crops are also at risk.

Getting a move on – could you go green?

Put all the cars in the world end to end, and they'd stretch around the Equator about 40 times. That's an awful lot of fossil fuel keeping their engines running. And an awful lot of filthy fumes being pumped out of their exhaust pipes. Serious about saving the planet? Why not decide to ditch your car and try a cleaner, greener way of getting from A to B?

Hop on a plane?

Flying uses tonnes and tonnes of fuel and dumps tonnes and tonnes of greenhouse gases into the atmosphere. And that's not all. The wiggly white lines planes leave in the sky are made when hot air from the engine mixes with cold air outside. Trouble is, they spread out in the sky to form clouds which stop heat escaping from the Earth.

Green rating: 0/5

Take the train?

Next time you're off on your yearly visit to Granny's, why not let the train take the strain? Trains are by far the greenest way to travel long distances, six times greener than planes. And some trains are super-speedy. Horribly high-tech magnetic trains in Japan can whizz along at speeds of up to 190 kilometres per hour. And you won't get stuck in a traffic jam.
Green rating: 3/5

Get on the bus?

But forget buses that burn fossil fuels. Brand-new buses are being built that run on cleaner, greener hydrogen gas. Instead of an engine, they've got a fuel cell like a battery where hydrogen mixes with oxygen to make electricity. In 2003, a car powered by hydrogen and solar power drove all the way across Australia. The only waste was water which was so pure you could slurp it down.
Green rating: 3/5

Get on your bike?

A brilliant way of nipping about and planet-friendly, too. Bikes can go for kilometres on a teeny teaspoon of oil and don't make a noise or mess. And all that fresh air and exercise is good for you. It's true. Make sure you know how to ride your bike safely, and if you get a new bike, don't forget to recycle your old, er, cycle.

Green rating: 4/5

Go for a walk?

It's the greenest way of getting out and about and it won't cost the Earth. All you need to do is drag yourself out of your armchair and put your best foot forward. You could even give your mum and dad the shock of their lives and leg it to school...

Green rating: 5/5

EIGHT TOP ENERGY-SAVING TIPS

1. *Don't leave stuff on standby.* Tellies and computers use about 85 per cent as much electricity as when they're switched on. Switch things off at the wall.

2. *Don't turn the central heating up.* Even if you're chilly. In fact, turn down the thermostat by just 1°C and you'll not only save energy but stop colossal amounts of carbon dioxide being pumped in the atmosphere. Put on a jumper instead.

3. *Do replace old light bulbs with special energy-saving ones*.* They use up to 80 per cent less energy than ordinary bulbs and last about 15 times longer. If you don't want to swap them all at once, start with the six bulbs you use the most.

4. *Don't fill the kettle to the brim.* Every time you want to make a cup of tea, only boil the number of cupfuls you actually need. You'll save enough energy to run a light bulb for several hours.

* Energy-saving bulbs contain mercury, so they should be disposed of properly and not just thrown in the bin. If one happens to break, you should leave the room for at least 15 minutes and wear gloves when picking up the broken bits.

5. *Do paint your house a different colour.* (Ask permission first.) It'll help your house heat up and cool down. Light colours reflect sunlight so paint it white in summer to keep it cool. Dark colours soak up sunlight so paint it black in winter for extra warmth.

6. *Do stop up any draughts.* It'll stop heat escaping and save energy. To test if your doors and windows are draughty, dangle a feather in front of them. If the feather flutters, it's time to seal up the cracks.

7. *Do hang washing outside.* Tumble dryers might be time-saving but they guzzle electricity. It's far greener to hang washing outside to dry. If you have to use a tumble dryer, make sure you squeeze most of the water out first.

8. *Don't throw old batteries away.* For starters, they contain dangerous chemicals which can leak and poison the soil. And making new batteries from scratch takes 50 times more energy than is in the batteries themselves. Use rechargeable batteries instead. With a battery charger, you can recharge them again and again.

A LOAD OF RUBBISH

It might sound like a load of rubbish, but horrible humans are turning the planet into an enormous litter bin. You might not even notice you're doing it, but you're probably chucking out your own weight in trash about every two months or so. Crisp packets, drinks cans, plastic bags, magazines ... the list goes on and on. And it's putting the planet in peril. Every time you bung something in the bin, you're wasting the precious materials it's made of and the energy used to make it. Especially as most of this rubbish isn't really rubbish at all and could be used all over again. Reckon it's all a lot of rot? Keep reading. This chapter's packed with planet-saving tips on how to turn trash into treasure.

FIVE RUBBISH FACTS

1 You and your family probably chuck out about a tonne of trash each year. That's enough to fill about 100 bin bags with around 150 metal cans, 100 glass bottles, two trees' worth of paper and twice your weight in old plastic. What a waste.

2 About three quarters of your rubbish ends up in a landfill site. It's dumped into a huge hole in the ground, then left to rot away. The hole is lined with clay and plastic to try to stop deadly chemicals seeping into the soil, and when it's full, it's covered over with soil. Trouble is, suitable sites for stinky landfills are running out fast.

3 Some rubbish is burned in gigantic ovens called incinerators. But burning is a, er, burning issue. True, it means less rubbish gets dumped into landfill sites. But burning also pumps filthy fumes and gases into the air and the leftover ash can be poisonous.

4 Stuff that's dumped in landfill sites can take months or even years to rot away. Orange peel takes around six months; a drinks can about 100 years and a plastic bag up to 1,000 years. And some things, like polystyrene, never, ever decay.

5 Until it closed down in 2001, gorily named Fresh Kills near New York City, USA, was the world's biggest rubbish dump. Its pile of trash stood taller than the Statue of Liberty. Fresh Kills has now been flattened and there are plans to turn it into a planet-friendly park.

SURVIVAL TIP

As rubbish rots away in landfill sites, it gives off methane and it's making an awful pong. But methane doesn't just smell terrible. It's also horribly explosive and a ghastly greenhouse gas. So why not pipe some of it off and use it to run a power station instead? That's what some dumps are doing, and it's definitely not a rubbish idea.

WHAT A LIBERTY!

Waste not, want not

The greenest way to stop the rot is cut down on waste. The three R's are three things you can do instead of simply chucking stuff away.

REDUCE IT

Next time you're going shopping, only buy things you really need. If you don't use it in the first place, you can't chuck it away. Can you? It's a case of less in, less out.

REUSE IT

So you've read the book and worn the T-shirt but don't just bin them straight away. Use them again or give them to a good cause like a charity.

RECYCLE IT

Drop your empty pop bottle in a recycling bin. It can be made into a brand-new bottle so the plastic won't go to waste. Recycling saves precious materials, energy and water.

Recycling files

Aluminium

- Aluminium's made from stuff called bauxite that's mined from rocks in the ground. To make one tonne of aluminium, you'll need to dig up four tonnes of bauxite.
- Aluminium's used for making drinks cans, tinfoil and foil tubs for takeaways.
- Every can that's recycled saves enough electricity to run the telly for three whole hours.
- To test if something's made from aluminium, scrunch it up. If it springs back into shape, it's not aluminium. (Crisp packets aren't aluminium, by the way.)
- Recycled foil can be used to make engine parts for cars.

Steel

- Steel's another metal that comes out of rocks in the ground. The rocks are blasted in a huge furnace to get the metal out.
- Scrap steel can be melted down and used again and again.
- To test if something's made from steel, try the magnet test. If it sticks, it's steel.
- If every office worker in Britain used one less staple a day, it would save a staggering 120 tonnes of steel.
- Your recycled baked bean can could end up as a bike frame, train track or part of a ship.

Paper

- Paper's made from pulped (mashed-up) pine trees. You probably chuck out about six trees' worth of paper every year.

- Making paper uses loads of energy and poisonous chemicals like the bleach used to turn paper white. It can get washed into rivers and seas, killing wildlife.

- Making recycled paper only uses up half the energy and water needed to make paper from scratch.

- It takes about a week to turn an old newspaper into today's news. You can also recycle magazines, paper bags, envelopes and cardboard.

- Milk and juice cartons are made from layers of cardboard sandwiched in between layers of plastic. They're pulped and the two bits separated out.

Glass

- Glass is made from sand, ash and limestone, melted down in huge ovens.
- Glass-making guzzles energy and digging up the sand spoils the landscape.
- Old glass can be crushed, then melted down and used again, and again, and again, and again. In fact, it never wears out.
- Recycling two glass bottles saves enough energy to make five cups of tea.
- Old glass bottles can be crushed and used to make new surfaces for roads and motorways and sand for golf courses.

Plastic

- Plastic doesn't rot away when it's dumped in landfill sites. Burning it's no better because it gives off poisonous fumes.
- Most plastic's made from oil. Recycling one tonne of plastic saves an awesome 2,600 litres of oil.
- Recycling one plastic drinks bottle saves enough energy to power a light bulb for six hours.
- Chewed-up toothbrushes tot up to about 45,000 tonnes of wasted plastic each year.
- Scientists are trying to produce plastics from sugar and potatoes that would rot away in a few months. But they're horribly costly to make.

Old and new mix and match

Recycled rubbish can be horribly useful. Try matching each of these six brand-new objects to the piece of old trash they're made from.

1 Fleecy jacket
2 Playground
3 Posh handbag
4 Pair of sandals
5 Street lights
6 Notepad

a) Elephant poo
b) Old plastic bags
c) Plastic drinks bottles
d) Old trainers
e) Spare tyres
f) Old CDs

Answers:

1c) It takes about 25 large drinks bottles to make a super-fluffy fleece. The plastic is chopped into flakes and melted, then it's pulled into long, thin threads. You spin the threads into yarn, then knit or weave your fleece out of it.

2 d) Millions of pairs of old trainers and other shoes are chucked in the bin each year. And they take a horribly long time to decay. So why not turn them into a kids' playground instead? That's exactly what famous sports shoe company Nike has being doing. They take old shoes, grind them up, then turn them into playgrounds and running tracks.

3 b) It's a case of bags to riches in India where old plastic bags are picked up from rubbish tips, washed and shaped into thick plastic sheets. The plastic's then cut into pieces and stitched into horribly posh handbags.

4 e) Getting rid of old car tyres is a big problem for the planet. For a start, they don't break down. And they can't be burned because they give off poisonous fumes. So what on Earth can you do with them? Try cutting up some spare tyres and turning them into sandals. Or fill them up with earth and cover them with concrete to make a cool skate park.

5 f) Most old CDs end up in landfill sites where they take ages to rot away. But a green-thinking company's now started recycling CDs and CD cases and turning them into burglar alarm boxes and street lighting.

6 a) You can turn all sorts of poo into paper, including elephant and rhino poo. And it doesn't even pong. Honestly. Here's what you need to do:

A) FIRST COLLECT YOUR ELEPHANT POO AND GIVE IT A GOOD RINSE. (THIS'LL LEAVE YOU WITH LOTS OF FIBRES FROM THE PLANTS THE ELEPHANTS MUNCHED FOR LUNCH.)

B) PUT THE FIBRES IN A BIG POT OF WATER AND BOIL IT UP FOR A FEW HOURS.

C) ADD SOME BANANA TREE OR PINEAPPLE PLANT FIBRES TO MAKE YOUR PAPER THICKER AND STRONGER AND GIVE EVERYTHING A REALLY GOOD MIX.

D) PAT LUMPS OF THE MIXTURE INTO WAFER-THIN SHEETS AND SPREAD THEM OVER A MESH. LEAVE THEM TO DRY IN THE SUN FOR A FEW HOURS.

E) PEEL THE SHEETS OF ELEPHANT-POO PAPER OFF THE MESH. YOU SHOULD GET ABOUT 25 LARGE SHEETS OF PAPER FROM ONE PILE OF POO.

HOMEWORK!

More rubbish ways of watching your waste

• *Stop using plastic bags*. Billions of bags get bunged in the bin, wasting millions of barrels of oil. These old bags take hundreds of years to decay and choke wild animals if they're washed into the sea. So next time you pop to the shops, take your own long-lasting bag with you.

• *Buy loose fruit and veg*. Not fruit and veg that's been packed in a polystyrene tray and wrapped up in plastic. True, packaging helps protect food and stops it getting squashed. But it also means that millions of tonnes of plastic, foam and polystyrene go to waste each year.

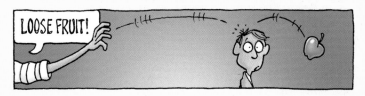

• *Get to the bottom of things*. If you've got a baby brother or sister, ask your mum to buy nappies that can be washed and used again. If she doesn't like the idea, bamboozle her with these green facts. Every day, millions of throwaway nappies are dumped in landfill sites where they use up lots of space and they take up to 500 years to rot away.

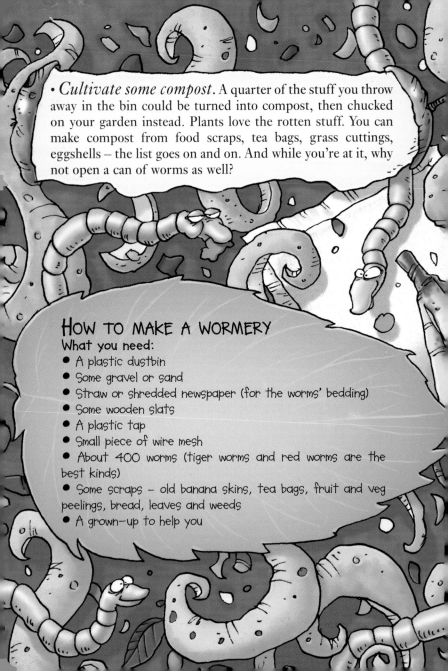

• *Cultivate some compost.* A quarter of the stuff you throw away in the bin could be turned into compost, then chucked on your garden instead. Plants love the rotten stuff. You can make compost from food scraps, tea bags, grass cuttings, eggshells – the list goes on and on. And while you're at it, why not open a can of worms as well?

HOW TO MAKE A WORMERY

What you need:

- A plastic dustbin
- Some gravel or sand
- Straw or shredded newspaper (for the worms' bedding)
- Some wooden slats
- A plastic tap
- Small piece of wire mesh
- About 400 worms (tiger worms and red worms are the best kinds)
- Some scraps – old banana skins, tea bags, fruit and veg peelings, bread, leaves and weeds
- A grown-up to help you

What you do:

1 Fix the tap into the outside of the bin near the bottom.

2 Place the wire mesh on the inside to stop the tap getting blocked up.

3 Drill some breathing holes into the lid of the bin.

4 Put a layer of sand and gravel in the bin.

5 Place the wooden slats over the sand and gravel.

6 Lay some bedding on top of the slats and put the worms on top.

7 Chuck in some scraps for the worms to munch. (Don't put more in until the worms have finished the first lot off.)

8 Leave it for a few weeks while the worms scoff the scraps. It'll pass through their bodies and get pushed out as rich, dark compost. You'll also get black, gooey liquid when you turn on the tap. You can use it as plant food.

• *Give your phone away*. Millions of mobile phones are thrown away each year. Most of them end up in landfill sites where they leak poisonous chemicals into the soil and water supply. Better to give your old phone to a charity so that someone else can use it instead. Why not e-cycle your computer and printer cartridges the same way?

• *Say it with flowers*. If you're going to a wedding, don't take plastic confetti to chuck at the happy couple. It'll still be hanging around in the landfill site years and years later. Choose confetti that'll rot away instead, like dried flower petals or recycled paper.

HORRIBLE HEALTH WARNING

It might sound horribly spooky but don't have to stop being green even when you're dead. For a start, you could choose a cardboard coffin that'll rot away in the ground. If you're dead set on wood, make sure it's from a forest where the trees are replaced as they're chopped down.

DOWN THE DRAIN

Most people take horrible H_2O (that's water, to you and me) for granted. You probably turn on the tap without giving it a second thought. But did you know that water is one of the planet's most precious resources? Why on Earth is it so wonderful? Well, it's vital for life, for a start. Without it, you'd die of thirst within a few days. And drinking isn't all water's useful for. We wash in it, water our fields with it, catch fish in it, make electricity from it (see page 33-34) and run our factories with it. And as there's no way of getting new water, you'd think we'd look after it, wouldn't you? But you'd be wrong. Horrible humans are pouring bucketloads of the stuff down the drain every day. Wat-er waste. And that's not all. Most of our drinking water comes from lakes and rivers and we're making a sickening mess of those. In some places, river water's so revoltingly rancid, it's poisonous for people to drink. Luckily, this chapter's chockfull of terrific tips for saving water and cleaning up your act. But before you leap into action, have you ever wondered where on Earth all this water comes from in the first place?

EARTH ALERT FILE

Name: WATER CYCLE
What is it: THE WAY THE EARTH'S WATER IS USED AGAIN AND AGAIN

HOW IT HAPPENS:

1 The Sun shines on the oceans, heating sea water up.

2 Sea water evaporates (turns into water vapour gas) and rises into the air.

3 As the water vapour rises, it cools down and condenses (turns back into liquid).

4 Billions of water droplets gang together to make a cloud.

5 The water droplets grow bigger and heavier until they fall as rain.

6 Some rain falls straight back into the sea. Some soaks into the ground. Some falls into rivers and streams that carry it back to the sea.

Water cycle facts:

• In the water cycle, the water on Earth's constantly on the move in the air, on the surface and underground.

• The rain you can see out of the window has fallen millions and millions of times before. That means it's the same rain that drenched the long—dead dinosaurs.

• By the time it reaches its 100th birthday, a water molecule has spent about 98 years in the ocean, 20 months as ice, two weeks in lakes and rivers and less than a week in the atmosphere.

• There's the same amount of water on Earth today as there was when the Earth formed. Trouble is, each year, millions more people are tapping into the water supply.

Could you be a hydrologist*?

*That's the posh name for a scientist who studies how water works. Fancy making a splash? Here are a few woefully watered-down facts it might be handy to know.

1 Scientists estimate there's a staggering 1,460 million cubic kilometres of water on Earth. That's 1,460,000,000,000,000,000,000 cubic metres – enough to fill a mind-boggling 700 million billion bathtubs.

2 Even though two thirds of the Earth's covered with water, most of it's salty and in the sea. Less than a paltry three per cent's fresh water we can drink. Trouble is, most of it's frozen in ice caps and glaciers or flowing along underground. So it's horribly hard to reach.

3 If you want a glass of water, you simply turn on the tap. Count yourself lucky. In poorer parts of the world, people often have to walk for many kilometres each day to collect their water from rivers and wells.

4 Water's good for you. Or is it? Over a billion (that's about one in every five) people on the planet don't have a clean, safe water supply. Their drinking water often comes straight from rancid rivers that are jam-packed with ghastly germs. These germs can spread deadly water-borne diseases like cholera and typhoid.

5 It's horribly hard to imagine how much water you use every day. For starters, you use about 80 litres when you have a bath and 100 litres when you run the washing machine. Not to mention about 10 litres every time you flush the loo. We use about 20 times more water than people did a thousand years ago. And people in richer countries use at least ten times as much water each day as people in poorer places.

6 An awful lot more water's used for farming and in factories. It takes about ten bathtubs of water to grow a 1-kg bag of

potatoes and three times as much for a bag of rice. And processing the materials needed to make a brand-new car uses a whopping 50 bathtubs.

HORRIBLE HEALTH WARNING

Global warming's making our water woes worse. It's messing up rainfall around the world, meaning some parts of the world are getting wetter and wetter, putting them at risk of fatal flooding. Other places are getting drier and suffering disastrous droughts. Both kinds of wild weather kill farmers' crops so horrible humans and animals go hungry.

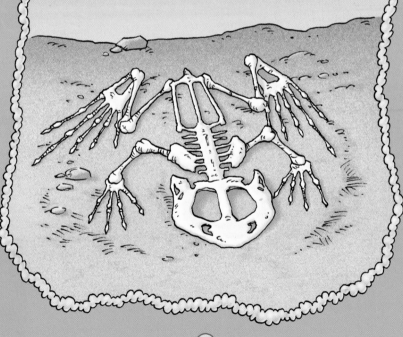

FOUR REASONS WHY RIVERS TURN RANCID

If you've got a raging river near you, check it out for signs of pollution. Dead giveaways are smelly water and flaked-out fish floating on the surface. Here's why some of our rivers are so rancid...

a) Stinking sewage

It usually goes to the sewage works where it's cleaned before it's pumped back into the river. But in some places, stinking sewage goes straight into rivers ... exactly as it is when you flush the loo or pull the plug after a bath. And you can't blame a fish for not wanting to flap around in that, can you?

b) Poisonous pesticides and fertilizers

These wash into rivers from farmers' fields when it rains. Trouble is, algae (tiny water plants) scoff down chemicals from the pesticides and fertilizers, then they grow and grow ... until they cover the water in thick, green slime. The slime blocks out sunlight which other plants need to make food. And when the algae die, they're gobbled up by bacteria which starve the water of oxygen ... so fish and other river creatures suffocate.

c) Filthy factory waste

Factories are often built near rivers so they can use the water supply. But they can also leak deadly chemicals and metals, such as copper and mercury. They're so horribly poisonous, fish don't stand a chance. Factories also pump whopping amounts of hot water into the river and the warmed-up river water runs low on oxygen.

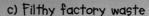

d) Odious oil

If odious oil spills into a slow-moving river, it forms a foul film across the surface. This stops oxygen getting into the water ... and you know the rest. On larger stretches of water, the oil clogs up birds' feathers so they can't stay warm or keep afloat, and they die. They also die when they try to clean their feathers and swallow the oil.

Five raging rivers at risk

Name: **Yangtze**
Location: **China**
Under threat from: **Pollution**
The mighty River Yangtze supplies nearly half of China's drinking water and two thirds of the water for growing vitally important rice. But so much sewage and rubbish is being dumped in the river, parts of it have been declared dead. Glass of dirty water, anyone?

Name: **Rio Grande**
Location: **USA/Mexico**
Under threat from: **Water extraction**
It's the second longest river in the USA and flows from Colorado to the Gulf of Mexico. But so much water's being pumped off for farms and cities, this once-raging river sometimes doesn't make it all the way to the sea.

Name: **Ganges**
Location: **India**
Under threat from: **Water extraction**
About half a billion people live on the Ganges floodplain and for them the river's a holy place. They believe bathing in the river will wash their sins away. Unfortunately, so much water's being taken for farmers' fields, this respected river is wasting away.

Name: **Nile**
Location: **Africa**
Under threat from: **Water extraction**
It's the longest river on Earth and its delta is home to some 80 million people. It's also an important breeding site for rare turtles and birds. Trouble is, despite its size, it's being so sapped of water it doesn't reach the sea in the dry season.

Name: **Indus**
Location: **Afghanistan, Pakistan, India, China**
Under threat from: **Climate change**
This raging river relies on glaciers high up in the Himalayas. And guess what? Climate change is beginning to bite. Warmer temperatures are melting the glaciers, cutting off the river's water supply.

EARTH—SHATTERING FACT

The River Thames in London used to be filthy. But over the last 50 years, it's really cleaned up its act. Its new sewers and water treatment plants work brilliantly ... usually. After serious storms they can overflow, dumping tonnes of stinking sewage in the river. The sewage chokes the water and can be fatal for fish. Luckily, two life-saving boats patrol the Thames, ready to act if oxygen levels dip. If this looks likely, they can inject up to 30 tonnes of oxygen into the water every day.

Watertight tips for saving water – the ins and outs

Inside…

• Don't leave the tap running when you're cleaning your teeth. While you're scrubbing your pearly white gnashers, you could be pouring up to 8 litres of water down the drain. Use a short burst of water to rinse your toothbrush and you'll save over two-thirds of the water you'd normally use.

• Do stick a brick in your toilet cistern. (Ask permission first.) A third of all the water you use at home is used to flush the loo. The brick will cut the amount of water you waste by two whole bathtubs a day. (In fact, old bathwater is brilliant for flushing the loo.)

• Do have a shower instead of bath. It's official. Giving up baths is good for the planet's health. Having a bath uses about 80 litres of water, while a shower uses only half as much. But don't soak in the shower for longer than three minutes – think you can manage that? And steer clear of power showers – they waste as much water as baths.

• Don't flush the loo after a wee. Wait until you do a poo. You'll save bucketloads of water that way. And speaking of things going down the pan… Never flush away things like cotton buds or nappies. They'll end up on beaches, ruining the view and harming wildlife.

• Do give your house a green clean. Cleaning stuff's chockfull of chemicals that can mess up water supplies (and pollute the air). So why not ditch the furniture polish and use a mixture of olive oil and vinegar instead. Use vinegar (again) sprinkled on scrunched-up newspaper to get your windows sparkling clean.
• Do put in a composting toilet. What happens is you go to the toilet and your poo collects in a box. In the box, the poo's broken down by bacteria and turned into compost you can chuck on your plants. When you've finished, drop a handful of straw or sawdust into the loo to stop the pong. OK, so it sounds horrible but the brilliant thing about this loo is it doesn't need water to wash the waste away. So you'll be flushed with success.

Outside…

• Do install a rain butt. Get a (recycled) plastic rain butt for your garden (it looks like a big plastic dustbin). Fix a tap to it and use the rainwater you collect to water your plants (or wash your dad's car). Early evening's the best time to pamper your plants because the water's less likely to evaporate in the Sun.

• Don't use a sprinkler to water the lawn. It can use up an eye-watering 640 litres of water an hour so imagine if you left it on all night. Use a watering can instead. In fact, grass only needs watering once a week if the weather's particularly dry. It doesn't matter if it goes a bit brown. It'll sprout up nice and green again next time it rains.

DINNER!

• Do leave grass cuttings on the lawn. They'll hold in the moisture, meaning you'll have to water your lawn less. Don't forget your flowerbeds. Bits of broken tree bark, coconut shells, or even shredded newspapers are brilliant at stopping the soil drying out.

• Don't waste your grey water. Grim-sounding grey water is the water you use for things like washing up and having a wash. Instead of throwing it down the drain, chuck it on your garden instead*. Hopefully, the plants won't mind the scummy bits on top.

*Don't use it on fruit and veg though, because of chemicals in washing-up liquid and toiletries.

SURVIVAL TIP

Places in dusty Australia are running out of water fast. But don't bother doing a rain dance. What about building some freaky peaks instead? Yep, a crackpot scientist suggested building a mountain range a colossal 2,000 kilometres long and 4 kilometres high. The idea was that moist air would rise to get over the mountain tops, cool into droplets and form rain clouds. So did this cliff-hanger scheme go ahead? Did it, heck! Talk about having your head in the clouds.

WIPED-OUT WILDLIFE

It's official. More kinds of wild animals and plants are becoming extinct (dying out for ever) than at any time in Planet Earth's history. And guess what? Yep, it's mostly down to horrible humans. Again. And we're wiping out our wildlife at an alarming rate. Worried scientists reckon more than 5,000 kinds of animals and 2,500 kinds of plants are under serious threat. It's true, animals have been dying out ever since life appeared on Earth millions of years ago. I mean, when was the last time you saw a dinosaur? Trouble is, right now it's happening much faster than ever before and our wildlife can't keep up. In the last few hundred years, we've waved bye-bye to dodos, passenger pigeons and Tasmanian wolves. And there's nothing we can do to bring them back. Now imagine a world without tigers, giant pandas, rhinoceroses and turtles. Sounds unbelievable? Sadly, they're all sliding towards extinction, too, and I bet they're wild about that.

FOUR REASONS WHY ANIMALS ARE UNDER ATTACK

They're losing their homes.

Wild places like rainforests, coral reefs and rivers are being taken over by horrible humans and cleared to make way for new homes, factories and farmland. So the animals that live there are forced to move out, or die. Pollution's another problem, particularly along the coast. Here, coral reefs are being suffocated by stinking sewage, and spilt oil is killing seabirds and other sea creatures.

They're attacked by alien animals.

No, they're not the kind of aliens that come from outer space. They're animals like foxes and rabbits humans used to take with them when they travelled to new places. The 'aliens' took over local animals' homes, and also ate them and their food. Rabbits were taken to Australia on settlers' ships hundreds of years ago. They're still spreading and eating so much grass it's leaving wild animals like kangaroos short of food.

They're being hunted to death.

Some animals are hunted for food, sport and luxuries. Thousands of elephants have been killed for their tusks, which are turned into ivory ornaments. Body parts from dead tigers and rhinos end up being used in traditional Chinese medicine. Birds like parrots and macaws are caught and sold as exotic pets. And some rare plants are in peril because they're being picked or dug up by plant collectors.

They can't stand the heat.

As the world gets warmer, some animals won't be able to cope. If they can't adapt to the changing conditions, they'll be wiped out. Simple as that. Scientist reckon up to a third of all animals and plants will die out if temperatures rise by just 2.5°C. And it's already happening. Pikas (they're cute creatures a bit like hamsters) like to live on cool mountain slopes in North America and Asia. They're dying out because they can't stand the heat.

SPOTTER'S GUIDE TO ENDANGERED* ANIMALS

* Warning note: Strictly speaking, these creatures are all critically endangered and that means they're one step away from being extinct. Blink and you might miss them.

Name: **Chinese alligator**
Appearance: Stocky, dark-green body. Up to 2 metres long.
Last known address: Yangtze River, China
Warning!!!
Horrible humans are draining the swamps and creeks where it likes to live. It's also killed because it likes to crunch farmers' ducks and dig its burrows in farmers' fields.
(Scientific name: Alligator sinensis)

These animals are all on the 2007 IUCN Red List of Threatened Species.

Name: **Bonin fruit bat**
Appearance: Long, black fur on its batty body. Foxy face.
Last known address: Five far-flung Japanese islands
Warning!!!
Its batty forest home is being chopped down for timber and
chomped by grazing goats. It's so rare no one knows for sure,
but it's reckoned there are only a few hundred bats left.
(Scientific name: Pteropus pselaphon)

Name: **Brazilian guitarfish**

Appearance: Flat, diamond-shaped body and long tail. Like a fishy guitar.

Last known address: Coast of southern Brazil

Warning!!!

Too many guitarfish are being caught before they've had chance to grow and breed. So stocks are perilously low and may soon have run out completely.

(Scientific name: Rhinobatos horkelii)

Name: **Philippine eagle**

Appearance: Dark brown and white feathers. Shaggy crest on head.

Last known address: Patches of tropical forest in the Philippines

Warning!!!

Its forest home is being cleared for farming and mining, disrupting its eggs and nests. It's also been hunted for food, and caught for putting on shows in zoos.

(Scientific name: Pithecophaga jefferyi)

Name: **Kouprey**
Appearance: Like a large ox with horns and big hump on its back.
Last known address: Forests and grasslands in Cambodia
Warning!!!
The last time anyone actually saw a kouprey alive was in 1988!
It's been hunted to death for its meat and its horn and skulls,
which are used in traditional Chinese medicine.
(Scientific name: Bos sauveli)

SURVIVAL TIP

But it's not all doom and gloom. Take the case of the golden lion
tamarin, a minuscule monkey with golden fur. About 1,200 of these
cute creatures live in patches of forest on the east coast of Brazil.

But it wasn't always the case. In the past, thousands of tamarins
were trapped for pets or left homeless when the forest was chopped
down. By 1970, a paltry 200 or so were left in the wild. Since then,
the tamarins have been bred in zoos and released back into wild.

EARTH ALERT FILE

Name: TROPICAL RAINFORESTS
What they are: EVERGREEN FORESTS GROWING NEAR
THE EQUATOR WHERE IT'S HOT AND WET ALL YEAR
ROUND

HOW THEY GROW:

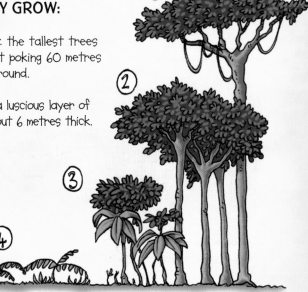

1 Emergents: the tallest trees
in the forest poking 60 metres
above the ground.

2 Canopy: a luscious layer of
treetops about 6 metres thick.

3 Understorey: smaller, shorter trees like palms and spindly
saplings.

4 Forest floor: the gloomy ground's covered in old, dead
leaves, mosses, fungi and ferns.

Rainforest facts:

● Bloomin' rainforests cover just 6 per cent of the Earth but they're home to half of all the plants and animals on the planet.

● The world-record rainforest grows along the banks of the awesome Amazon River in South America. It's almost as big as the whole of Australia.

● Scientists have counted at least one million kinds of rainforest insects and there may be millions more.

● Rainforests are in serious danger. All over the world, they're facing the axe. A soccer-pitch sized patch of forest is being chopped down EVERY BLOOMIN' SECOND.

Could you rescue a rainforest?

You'll need to get to grips with some rotten rainforest facts first.

1 Rainforests have been around for ages. Some are as old as:
a) The pyramids
b) The dinosaurs
c) The Romans

2 How many different kinds of plants and animals would you find in a patch of rainforest the size of a soccer pitch?
a) 50
b) 5
c) 500

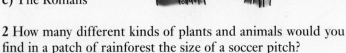

3 Rainforest plants help doctors to treat:
a) Coughs and colds
b) Leukaemia
c) Frostbite

ARH-CHOO!

4 Why are the rainforests being cut down?
a) For timber
b) For farmland
c) For grazing cattle

5 Each year, we're chopping down rainforest the size of:
a) Switzerland
b) 60 soccer pitches
c) Your school

6 How do rainforests change the climate?
a) By soaking up rainfall
b) By soaking up greenhouse gases
c) By pumping out greenhouse gases

MY DAYS OF DOING ANYTHING ARE OVER!

Answers:
1 b) The first rainforests on the planet grew about 300 million years ago. They were packed with tree-sized shrubs like tree ferns and horsetails that dinosaurs loved to munch. Excited scientists recently found a fossilized rainforest in an underground coal mine.

2 c) Pick any patch of rainforest and it's likely to be teeming with life. The Amazon rainforest alone is home to over a quarter of the world's kinds of birds. Sadly, as the rainforests go up in smoke, millions of plants and animals are being wiped out.

SAVE OUR HOMES!

3 b) More than a third of the medicines we use have

ingredients from rainforest plants. Take the rosy periwinkle from Madagascar. It contains chemicals doctors use to treat the deadly disease leukaemia (that's a kind of cancer of the blood).

4 a), b) and **c)** Rainforests are facing the chop because of valuable timber from hardwood trees. They're also cleared to make room for people to grow crops. And next time you scoff a burger, spare a thought for how it reached you. Huge parts of the Amazon rainforest have been turned into grazing for beef cattle.

5 a) Alarming, isn't it? In Thailand, over three quarters of the country's rainforests have been cut down in the last 40 years. And once they're gone, they can't grow back. At this rate, there won't be any bloomin' rainforest left in another 50 years' time.

6 a), b) and **c)** Rainforest trees soak up millions of tonnes of carbon dioxide, as they grow (see page 13). And fewer rainforests means less carbon dioxide's absorbed. And when the trees are burned, they release millions more tonnes of carbon dioxide into the atmosphere. Rainforests also soak up rain and let it flow slowly into rivers and streams. Once they're gone, there's nothing to stop ferocious flooding.

I LOVE A GOOD SHOWER!

Six tough tips for saving wildlife

Stop scoffing crisps.
Stuff called palm oil is used to make crisps and it's grown on huge palm-oil farms. (It's also in hair conditioner, soap, biscuits – the list goes on and on.) Trouble is, the farms are built on chopped-down rainforest where the orang-utans used to live. And it's got so bad that if nothing's done, it could be curtains for orang-utans in the next ten years.

Go for green wood.
Hardwoods comes from tropical trees like teak and mahogany that bloom in rainforests. They're used to make posh furniture, and they're the main reason rainforests are at risk. If you're after a nice new table, choose one made from wood like pine, ash or beech that comes from a sustainable forest.

To be greener still, branch out and buy a bamboo table instead.

Stick to seaside rock.
If you're bringing back a souvenir from your hols, make it a stick of rock. Never buy anything made from rare wildlife like crocodile-skin handbags or snakeskin belts. Steer clear of jewellery made from ivory, tortoiseshell or coral. Coral comes from reefs that protect places on the coast from storms, and they're at serious risk.

Be picky about fish.

Next time you're chomping on fish and chips, check what sort of fish you're eating. You know the saying 'There's plenty of fish in the sea'? Well, it isn't true, I'm afraid. So many fish are being caught that stocks of some kinds are  running out. The chips are down for Atlantic cod, halibut and salmon, shark, monkfish, tuna and plaice. So how about trying some pollock, hoki, red mullet or cuttlefish instead?

Go on holiday.

If you want to watch wildlife, why not set off on safari. In poor countries, especially, the money you spend on your holiday can help protect threatened animals. So you can enjoy the trip of a lifetime while doing your bit for the planet. But pick your trip carefully or you could do more harm than good. (Don't forget to plant a tree when you get back to balance out all those greenhouses gases your plane's given off.)

Dig a garden pond.

(Ask permission first.)

It's a brilliant way of bringing wildlife into your back yard. Here's what you need to do:

a) Choose a sunny spot, away from overhanging trees.
b) Get digging. The sides should be sloping with the deepest bit in the middle.
c) Cover the bottom with old newspapers or an old carpet.
d) Line the whole hole with a plastic sheet and add a layer of soil on top.
e) Fill your pond with water.
f) Add plants to put oxygen in the water.
g) Now sit back and wait for some pond-loving frogs, toads and insects to start moving in.
h) Once your pond is established (after about a year) you could add some pond creatures like snails and sticklebacks.

EPILOGUE

Congratulations! You've come face to face with the perils facing Planet Earth and you're well on your way to going a ghastly shade of green. But before you start digging up your dad's flowerbeds to grow your own veg, here's a word of warning. You might have made a green-fingered start but there's still a horribly long way to go. The Planet's in serious trouble and we've got no one else to blame but ourselves. So what do you do if global warming really turns up the heat despite everything you've gone and done? Don't panic. Here are some last-ditch survival tips. Well, what have you got to lose?

Five red-hot survival tips
(if you've tried everything else and failed)

1 *Float your house*. With sea levels on the up, it seems a sensible way to go. Floating houses are already being lived in in the Netherlands where the low-lying land's in serious danger of being submerged. Who knows where they might catch on next?

2 *Slurp a glass of fog*. People in Chile's bone-dry Atacama Desert collect water from the fog rolling in off the sea. The fog's caught in large nets and condenses (turns into water). If you live near the coast, why not try this at home when water shortages kick in?

3 *Paint everything white*. Some cities like Los Angeles are already painting their roads. White reflects sunlight back into space and cools the planet down. That's one of the reasons we've got the perishing poles. Steer clear of dark colours. They'll keep heat in.

4 *Give the air a good scrub*. But forget using a piddling scrubbing brush. You'll need some huge towers shaped like fly-swatters sticking out of the ground. They'll suck up poisonous carbon dioxide which you'll have to bury somewhere underground.

5 *Adopt an orang-utan*. Better still, set up your own orang sanctuary. You'll need a patch of rainforest to put it in – if there's any left, that is. And don't forget animals like chimpanzees, gorillas and elephants – they're all under threat.

You might think what's the point? Adopting orang-utans is all very well but you can't save the whole bloomin' planet on your own. Is going green really worth all the bother? The answer is 'yes, it is'! Here's the good news… By making horribly small changes to the way you live, you can cut your carbon footprint by tonnes each year. And you're not alone. If even a million people follow in your green footsteps, we'd be talking an awful lot of gruesome greenhouse gases saved. Governments and conservation groups all over the world are also working hard to stop the rot. And the bad news? Well, saving the planet isn't going to be easy but fingers crossed going green does the trick. If not, polar bears and pandas might not be only ones in peril…

Wicked world-saving websites

If you're interested in finding out more about **saving the planet**, here are some websites to check out:

www.carboncalculator.co.uk
Follow the instructions to work out your carbon footprint.

www.carbonfootprint.com/calculator.html

www.foe.co.uk
The Friends of the Earth website, packed with environmental information.

www.recyclezone.co.uk
Facts about things you can recycle.

www.panda.org
The Worldwide Fund for Nature's website with fact sheets about climate change, endangered species, marine life, pollution and much, much more.

www.ypte.org.uk
The Young People's Trust for the Environment helps young people to understand the problems facing the planet and the need for green living.

www.iucnredlist.org
The annual list produced by the World Conservation Union giving details of the plants and animals at greatest risk of becoming extinct.

www.solarcooking.org
Everything you ever wanted to know about solar cooking.

INDEX

Enjoyed
PLANET IN PERIL?
Want to get your teeth
into more Horrible
Geography Handbooks?
WILD ANIMALS &
WICKED WEATHER
are in the shops
NOW!